KNOWLEDGE FROM GOD ALMIGHTY
VOLUME 1
Davante Farmer

BUMBLEMEYER
PUBLICATIONS

https://bumblemeyer.com

Table of Contents

Chapter 1
The Lack of Knowledge of Sin

The Bible says in Hosea 4:6 that the Lord our God said:

>"My people are destroyed from a lack of knowledge.

>Because you have rejected knowledge,

>I also reject you as my priests;

>because you have ignored the law of your God,

>I also will ignore your children."

In Hosea 6:6, the Lord our God said,

>"For I desire mercy, not sacrifice,

>and acknowledgement of God rather than burnt offerings."

And in Matthew 22:29, the Lord Jesus said to the people who asked Him a question about marriage in the afterlife, "You are in error because you do not know the Scriptures or the power of God."

You see, quite often we are in error about what is right and wrong because we do not know the Scriptures (the ancient texts) or the power of

God. We do not know the Scriptures like we ought to know them. We might get—we might understand—a piece here and a piece there every now and again, but even I must admit the truth that I sometimes overlook the main points when I read Scripture, and I, too, am in error because I do not know the Scriptures or the power of God like I should.

There is always something we miss despite the fact all the ancient texts—not only the Bible—teach about sin, judgment, righteousness, and the afterlife. For now, however, the most important thing we need to understand is what is meant by "sin."

Sin, as defined in the Oxford English Dictionary, is an immoral act considered to be a transgression against Divine Law.

To be in sin is to do the opposite of what God Almighty requires of us.

To be in sin is to be disobedient to a set of Commandments God Almighty instituted for our own benefit as humankind and as a society.

If we live according to God's Word, *His* commands, *His* directions, and *His* laws that He has clearly laid out for our lives, things start going right. In the same way, when we are being disobedient and are not living according to God's Word, things will start going wrong.

Psalms 119:9 says, "How can a young person stay on the path of purity? By living according to Your Word."

AMEN!

To turn away from God's Word to the right or to the left is like driving a car on the sidewalk when it belongs in the street, or like walking in the middle of the street when the sidewalk is much safer. Some folks do like to do crazy things! But to stay on the pure path, you need God's Word for direction and enlightenment.

Without God's Word, we are lost without any direction.

In Romans 6:23, brother Paul says, "For the wages of sin is death, but the gift of God is eternal life in Christ Jesus our Lord."

But how do we know if we are in sin?

Most of the time people are in sin and do not know it, but they *can* feel it. We have a conscience that bears witness itself through our spirit. We can feel it when we are wrong and when we are right, deep down on the inside.

Anger, hatred, jealousy, selfish ambition, dissension, fits of rage, malice, deceit, greed, witchcraft, horoscopes, occult practices, adultery, sexual immorality, impurity, drunkenness, orgies, pride, instigating conflict or violence in the community, stealing, haughtiness, lying (false witness), coveting (desiring something that does not belong to you): ALL of this is sin. A lot of people do not want to talk about sin or even admit it, but it is necessary to acknowledge sin in your life; it is very important and what the Lord wishes us to understand and recognize—this is why He sent His Word.

The wages of sin is death!

In Psalms 107:20, David says,

> "He sent out His Word and healed them;
>
> He rescued them from the grave."

In 1 John 1:5-10, Brother John said,

"This is the message we have heard from Him and declare to you: God is light; in Him there is no darkness at all. If we claim to have fellowship with Him and yet walk in the darkness, we lie and do not live out the Truth. But if we walk in the light, as He is in the light, we have fellowship with one another, and the blood of Jesus, His Son, purifies us from all sin.

"If we claim to be without sin, we deceive ourselves and the Truth is not in us. If we confess our sins, He is faithful and just and will forgive us our sins and purify us from all unrighteousness. If we claim we have not sinned, we make Him out to be a liar and His Word is not in us."

You see, if we claim to have fellowship with God but go on living in spiritual darkness, then we are lying to ourselves and not practicing the Truth. But if we are living in the Light as God is in the Light, then we are in fellowship and the blood of Jesus cleanses us.

If we declare we have no sin, we are only lying to ourselves and are not living in the Truth. But if we confess our sins, He will cleanse us from all our wickedness.

If we declare we have no sin, we are calling God Almighty a liar, showing Him that His Word has no place in our hearts. To go against God and anything He has commanded or said in the past, present, or future is a sin. To go against His Word is to be in sin.

From ancient times, God Almighty has left a set of commands for us to follow. He has used whomever in whatever way He wishes to speak to us.

In Exodus 3:1-22, God Almighty spoke to Moses through a Burning

Bush—it was literally on fire yet the bush was not consumed.

In Numbers 22:21-39, God Almighty spoke to Balaam through a donkey.

In Luke 19:28-44, the Lord Jesus stopped at the Mount of Olives on His way to Jerusalem, and when His disciples, in their excitement, called out praises, some Pharisees asked Him to command the disciples be quiet. Jesus states, "I tell you, if they keep silent, the stones will cry out [in praise]."

God Almighty can speak through whomever and whatever He wishes. He uses kings and queens, leaders, pharaohs, lowly people, angels, etc. In Genesis 41:41-57, the Lord used the Pharoah of Egypt to place Joseph in charge of all of Egypt to save his family. And for nearly 2,000 years, the Lord has spoken to us through His Son, Jesus Christ.

Not all of the pharaohs, kings, queens, leaders, and lowly people God Almighty chose to speak to us were good, and not all of them were bad. They were, like us, human beings, even if we sometimes look at them as gods. They made mistakes, like we do. But they were God's servants sent to carry out His will and to teach us. People like Moses, whom God chose to lead His people out of Egypt. Moses never entered the Promised Land because he was disobedient (Deuteronomy 32:51-52). Like us, Moses was a sinner, yet God still chose him to give us a set of Commandments, a set of Holy Laws for us to follow, to guide us.

I promise you, when we follow these Laws with our heart, we will be blessed. Things start going right. Quite often, when things are going wrong around us, it is because we are doing something directly in opposition to

God's Word, in opposition to what God Almighty has commanded, and that is sin. We may not even realize we are doing something wrong.

Exodus 20:1-17 provides us with God's Commandments as follows:

"You shall have no other gods before me.

"You shall not make for yourself an image in the form of anything in heaven above or on the earth beneath or in the waters below. You shall not bow down to them or worship them; for I, the Lord your God, am a jealous God, punishing the children for the sin of the parents to the third and fourth generation of those who hate me, but showing love to a thousand generations of those who love me and keep my commandments.

"You shall not misuse the name of the Lord your God, for the Lord will not hold anyone guiltless who misuses his name.

"Remember the Sabbath day by keeping it holy. Six days you shall labor and do all your work, but the seventh day is a sabbath to the Lord your God. On it you shall not do any work, neither you, nor your son or daughter, nor your male or female servant, nor your animals, nor any foreigner residing in your towns. For in six days the Lord made the heavens and the earth, the sea, and all that is in them, but He rested on the seventh day. Therefore the Lord blessed the Sabbath day and made it holy.

"Honor your father and your mother, so that you may live long in the land the Lord your God is giving you.

"You shall not murder.

"You shall not commit adultery.

"You shall not steal.

"You shall not give false testimony against your neighbor.

"You shall not covet your neighbor's house. You shall not covet your neighbor's wife, or his male or female servant, his ox or donkey, or anything that belongs to your neighbor."

These Ten Commandments were a lifeline for the Hebrews more than 3,000 years ago. Nearly 1,500 years later, our Lord and Savior Jesus confirmed their importance, as recorded in Matthew 5:17, "Do not think that I have come to abolish the Law or the Prophets; I have not come to abolish them but to fulfill them."

Now, listen to what our brother Paul says in Romans 3:20-24:

"Therefore no one will be declared righteous in God's sight by the works of the Law; rather, through the Law we become conscious of our sin.

"But now apart from the Law the righteousness of God has been made known, to which the Law and the Prophets testify. This righteousness is given through faith in Jesus Christ to all who believe. There is no difference between Jew and Gentile, for all have sinned and fall short of the glory of God, and all are justified freely by His grace through the redemption that came by Jesus Christ."

You see, the Law shows us the sin in our life. Yet, as brother Paul says in Romans 6:23, "For the wages of sin is death, but the gift of God is eternal life in Christ Jesus our Lord." God Almighty made a Way for us to escape the death caused by our sin. Through our acceptance of His Son

Jesus Christ as our Lord and Savior, God gifts us with eternal life.

In Matthew 22:35-40, the Pharisees approached Jesus: "One of them, an expert in the Law, tested Him with a question: 'Teacher, which is the greatest commandment in the Law?' Jesus replied: 'Love the Lord your God with all your heart and with all your soul and with all your mind.' This is the first and greatest commandment. And the second is like it: 'Love your neighbor as yourself.' All the Law and the Prophets hang on these two commandments."

In quoting Deuteronomy 6:5 and Leviticus 19:18, Jesus provides a summary of the Ten Commandments as given to the Hebrews through Moses: the first four combined in the "first and greatest" Commandment showing how to love and honor God, the remaining six combined in the second Commandment indicating how we are to treat others.

Christianity, like Judaism, recognizes the Ten Commandments but focus is placed on the summary provided by Jesus. As recorded in John 13:34-35, Jesus said, "A new Command I give you: Love one another. As I have loved you, so you must love one another. By this everyone will know that you are My disciples, if you love one another."

Before we continue our study of sin as it applies to Christianity, we need to explore the concepts of sin and salvation according to other cultures of the ancient world.

Other religious faiths have similar laws their believers are supposed to follow. For Islam, while they do not accept the authority of the Bible other than as an earlier revelation by God, they do believe Moses was a Prophet. But to achieve salvation, a person must not sin and must perform good deeds. Since humans find it impossible not to sin, they must repent and seek God's mercy. Repenting, however, does not mean you can continue to sin.

The rules of behavior found in the Ten Commandments appear as a list eight prohibitions in the Islamic holy text—specifically Qur'an 6:151-153[1]:

> "Say, come, I will recite what God has made a
> sacred duty for you: Ascribe nothing as equal
> with God.
> Be good to your parents.
> You shall not kill your children on a plea of want;
> we provide sustenance for you and for them.
> You shall not approach lewd behavior whether
> open or in secret.
> You shall not take life, which God has made
> sacred, except by way of justice and law. Thus
> does God command you, that you may learn
> wisdom.
> And you shall not approach the property of the
> orphan, except to improve it, until he attains the
> age of maturity.
> Give full measure and weight, in justice; no
> burden should be placed on any soul but that
> which it can bear.
> And if you give your word, do it justice, even if a
> near relative is concerned; and fulfill your

obligations before God. Thus does God

command you, that you may remember."

In Hinduism, there are six deadly sins called the *Arishdavardas* or, "six enemies of the mind" that prevent a believer's soul from escaping the cycle of birth and death[2]:

Kama (desire)

Krodha (anger)

Lobha (greed)

Moha (delusion)

Mada (arrogance)

Matsarya (envy/jealousy)

Hinduism shares its main beliefs with Buddhism, Jainism, and Sikhism in which the soul must suffer an endless cycle of birth and death until they achieve Moksha, or liberation. To achieve Moksha, there are many different "disciplines" a person must perform, including yoga and meditation[3].

Even the ancient Egyptians understood sin. In fact, Egyptians had forty-two deadly sins, known as the Negative Confession in the Book of the Dead, which some consider the Egyptian version of a bible[4]. At death, the soul of the dead person met with the god Osiris in the Hall of Truth for judgment. The heart—which was considered part of the soul—was placed on a scale to be weighed against the goddess Maat's white Feather of Truth. While the heart was weighed, the soul recited the Negative Confession and the god Thoth recorded the responses. Though each person's Negative Confession depended on what work they did when alive, following is one example of what the Egyptians considered important[5]:

I have not committed sin.

I have not committed robbery with violence.

I have not stolen.

I have not slain men or women.

I have not stolen grain.

I have not purloined offerings.

I have not stolen the property of God.

I have not uttered lies.

I have not carried away food.

I have not uttered curses.

I have not committed adultery.

I have made none to weep.

I have not eaten the heart.

I have not attacked any man.

I am not a man of deceit.

I have not stolen cultivated land.

I have not been an eavesdropper.

I have not slandered anyone.

I have not been angry without just cause.

I have not debauched the wife of any man.

I have not debauched the wives of other men.

I have not polluted myself.

I have terrorized none.

I have not transgressed the Law.

I have not been angry.

I have not shut my eyes to the Word of Truth.

I have not blasphemed.

I am not a man of violence.

I have not been a stirrer of strife.

I have not acted in undue haste.

I have not pried into other's matters.

I have not multiplied my words in speaking.

I have wronged none, I have done no evil.

I have not worked witchcraft against the King.

I have never stopped the flow of water of a neighbor.

I have never raised my voice.

I have never cursed God.

I have not acted with arrogance.

I have not stolen the bread of the gods.

I have not carried away the knenfu cakes from the spirits of the dead.

I have not snatched away the bread of the child, nor treated with contempt the god of my city.

I have not slain the cattle belonging to the god.

Yet even with this confession, it was the weight of the heart that would decide a soul's final fate. If the heart weighed more than the feather, the god Amut ate it and the soul was doomed to remain in the underworld. If the heart was lighter than or the same weight as Maat's feather, the soul was allowed into paradise, known as the Field of Reeds. In some cases, however, the soul went on a dangerous journey before reaching paradise and a copy of the Book of the Dead was buried with them to provide any spells they might need on this journey[6].

For the ancient Greeks, there were seven "evil thoughts"—or "deadly sins"—addressed in their mythology[7]:

Gluttony—consumed by their own appetites

Lust—consumed by sexual desire

Greed—consumed by desire for wealth and possessions

Pride—the root cause of all other sins

Jealousy—consumed by resentment or bitterness towards others

Wrath—consumed by their own rage

Sloth (laziness)—consumed by a lack of ambition

As we see, no matter the culture, sin is defined as an immoral act; a transgression that goes against a human law, a rule, or a code of conduct; and an offense against divine Law. But how did sin come into the world?

In Romans 5:12-14, brother Paul says,

"Therefore, just as sin entered the world through one man, and death through sin, and in this way death came to all people, because all sinned—

"To be sure, sin was in the world before the law was given, but sin is not charged against anyone's account where there is no law. Nevertheless, death reigned from the time of Adam to the time of Moses, even over those who did not sin by breaking a command, as did Adam, who is a pattern of the one to come."

Paul continues in Romans 5:17, "For if, by the trespass of the one man, death reigned through that one man, how much more will those who receive God's abundant provision of grace and of the gift of righteousness reign in life through the one man, Jesus Christ!"

The wages of sin is death—Adam and Eve, once they disobeyed God, would suffer. Expelled from the Garden of Eden, separated from God, they would have to make their way in a changed world, one filled with unknown dangers, disease, and pain. They would now grow old and weak, and eventually die.

Cain took his parents' fall from grace one step further when he killed his brother. And so the cycle continued.

In Proverbs 6:16-19, brother Solomon warns,

> "There are six things the Lord hates,
>
> seven that are detestable to him:
>
> haughty eyes,
>
> a lying tongue,
>
> hands that shed innocent blood,
>
> a heart that devises wicked schemes,
>
> feet that are quick to rush into evil,
>
> a false witness who pours out lies,
>
> and a person who stirs up conflict in the community."

Brother Samuel tells Saul in 1 Samuel 15:22-23:

> "Does the Lord delight in burnt offerings and sacrifices
>
> as much as in obeying the Lord?
>
> To obey is better than sacrifice,

and to heed is better than the fat of rams.

For rebellion is like the sin of divination,

and arrogance like the evil of idolatry.

Because you have rejected the word of the Lord,

he has rejected you as king."

Nobody wins in a life of sin.

Sin is immoral: bad, wrongful, evil, wicked, dishonest, dishonorable, unfair, impure, devious, shameless, perverted, lustful, shady, crooked, and corrupt. It is a transgression against Divine Law. Sin is wrongdoing, crime, wickedness, immorality, profanity, ungodliness, unrighteousness, and evildoing. It is because of sin that the world is in bad shape, that we are in bad shape. Because of sin we have been separated from God.

In Isaiah 59:1-2, brother Isaiah says, "Surely the arm of the Lord is not too short to save, nor is His ear too dull to hear. But your iniquities have separated you from your God; your sins have hidden His face from you so that He will not hear."

And in Ecclesiastes 9:18, brother Solomon states, "Wisdom is better than weapons of war; but one sinner destroys much good."

Nobody wins in a life of sin.

Brother Paul states in Galatians 5:19-21:

> "The acts of the flesh are obvious: sexual immorality, impurity and debauchery; idolatry and witchcraft; hatred, discord, jealousy, fits of rage, selfish ambition, dissensions, factions and envy; drunkenness, orgies, and the like. I warn you, as I did before, that those who live like this will not inherit the kingdom of God."

Everything Paul lists is sin.

Murder, unjust anger, greed, unfair judgment, harsh criticism, gossip, coarse jokes, slander, lust over things that are not yours: ALL this is sin.

God Almighty gave us Ten Commandments to obey for our own good. To break any of these Laws is sin, yet we break His Laws daily. Much of the time, we do not even know we are sinning against Him. Between television, radio, the Internet, smartphones, movies, newspapers, magazines, even books, we are constantly battered and trapped by temptation, fear, jealousy, anger, and greed.

Our sin affects others. My sin affects me, and not only me but also the people around me, especially the ones I sin against. Most importantly, my sin can affect my relationship with the Lord our God.

Now, you need to understand I can never hurt God Almighty; no one can, but He does have feelings. Most of His feelings are expressed to us through His love. He loves us; God Almighty truly loves us. Look to your left and to your right and tell me what you see: PEOPLE—mankind—brothers, sisters, mothers, fathers, cousins, aunts, uncles, nieces, nephews, friends. PEOPLE—Black, White, Hispanic, Latino, Korean, Chinese, Indian, Mexican, African, Greek, Egyptian, Russian, and so forth. It does not matter who you are, what race or ethnic group you come from. God loves ALL of us.

In Genesis 1:26-27, Moses wrote that the Lord God said,

> "Let Us (The Father, The Son, and The Holy Spirit) make mankind in Our image, in Our likeness, so that they may rule over the fish in the sea and the birds in the sky ... So God created mankind in His

own image, in the image of God He created them; male and female He created them."

You see, God created us, all mankind, in His image.

Though we cannot see Him, we are told we look like Him, all of us. I have never seen God Almighty in His truest form, His whole Deity. I cannot see Him even if I want to.

As Paul said in 1 Timothy 6:15-16, "... God, the blessed and only Ruler, the King of kings and Lord of lords, who alone is immortal and who lives in unapproachable light, whom no one has seen or can see. To Him be honor and might forever. Amen."

In Romans 1:20, brother Paul said, "For since the creation of the world God's invisible qualities—His eternal power and divine nature—have been clearly seen, being understood from what has been made, so that people are without excuse."

Listen, the wind is real—I can breathe it every day though I cannot see it, for it is invisible.

Oxygen is real—we breathe it in but cannot see it, for it is invisible.

So, while we cannot see God because He is invisible, we know He is real from what we see and feel around us.

In 1 John 4:20-21, brother John states,

> "Whoever claims to love God yet hates a brother or sister is a liar. For whoever does not love their brother and sister, whom they have seen, cannot love God, whom they have not seen. And He has given us this command: Anyone who loves God must also love their brother and sister."

We can never hurt God Almighty, but the closest we can get to hurting God is by hurting our brothers and sisters, which we do daily. And that is sin.

We are all brothers and sisters, and we should be acting like it.

We are all made in the image of God and we are all special to Him. So why are we not special to each other?

Remember what Jesus says in Matthew 22:37-40: "Love the Lord your God with all your heart and with all your soul and with all your mind. This is the first and greatest commandment. And the second is like it: Love your neighbor as yourself. All the Law and the Prophets hang on these two commandments."

Paul reminds us of this in Romans 13:8-10:

> "Let no debt remain outstanding, except the continuing debt to love one another, for whoever loves others has fulfilled the law. The commandments, 'You shall not commit adultery,' 'You shall not murder,' 'You shall not steal,' 'You shall not covet,' and whatever other command there may be, are summed up in this one command: 'Love your neighbor as yourself.' Love does no harm to a neighbor. Therefore love is the fulfillment of the Law."

Now, if I am not acting the way I know I should act and not doing the right thing, I am sinning, as James says in James 4:17: "If anyone, then, knows the good they ought to do and doesn't do it, it is sin for them."

I know when I am wrong. I know what I ought to do and how I should act. I know when I have sinned. But if I say I am not a sinner, I know better, because as brother John says in 1 John 1:8-10:

"If we claim to be without sin, we deceive ourselves and the truth is not in us. If we confess our sins, He (God Almighty) is faithful and just and will forgive us our sins and purify us from all unrighteousness. If we claim we have not sinned, we make Him out to be a liar and His Word is not in us."

In Matthew, John the Baptist gives us the recipe to turn from sin—repent and confess. Matthew 3:1-2 states, "In those days John the Baptist came, preaching in the wilderness of Judea and saying, 'Repent, for the kingdom of heaven has come near.'"

In Matthew 3:8 and 3:10, brother John cautions the Pharisees and Sadducees: "Produce fruit in keeping with repentance … The ax is already at the root of the trees, and every tree that does not produce good fruit will be cut down and thrown into the fire."

In Acts 2:38-39, brother Peter tells a crowd of people, " … Repent and be baptized, every one of you, in the name of Jesus Christ for the forgiveness of your sins. And you will receive the gift of the Holy Spirit. The promise is for you and your children and for all who are far off—for all whom the Lord our God will call."

Once I accept I am wrong and that God Almighty and His Word are right, I can freely confess my sins to God through Jesus Christ, and am enabled by the Holy Spirit to freely accept the Truth and be saved:

I have sinned by doing wrong to you and others!

I confess this openly to those I hurt!

In James 5:16, brother James says:

"Therefore confess your sins to each other and pray for each other that you may be healed. The prayer of a righteous person is powerful and effective." AMEN!

In Titus 2:12-13, brother Titus explains:

"It [the grace of God] teaches us to say 'No' to ungodliness and worldly passions, and to live self-controlled, upright and godly lives in this present age, while we wait for the blessed hope—the appearing of the glory of our great God and Savior, Jesus Christ ..."

In Acts 16:31-34, brother Paul and Silas tell their jailer, who has asked what he must do to be saved: " ... Believe in the Lord Jesus, and you will be saved—you and your household", after which the two men share the Word of God with the jailer, his family, and his servants:

"At that hour of the night the jailer took them and washed their wounds; then immediately he and all his household were baptized. The jailer brought them into his house and set a meal before them; he was filled with joy because he had come to believe in God—he and his whole household."

So, as a result of Adam and Eve's disobedience in the Garden of Eden, sin came into the world. From that point forward, we have been born into sin, which is why we die. Brother David says in Psalms 51:5, "Surely I was sinful at birth, sinful from the time my mother conceived me." It is not old age, however, that is the reason for death. It is because sin rots us away from the inside out. And sin disqualifies us from entering into the afterlife.

Then, what do we do? How can we change this outcome?

ALL WE HAVE TO DO IS ACCEPT **JESUS CHRIST** AS OUR **LORD** AND **SAVIOR**!

THAT'S IT!

Without Jesus Christ and the approval God placed in Him, we cannot be saved.

Without Jesus Christ, we cannot enter into God's Kingdom.

We are saved from God Almighty's wrath and judgment from sin through faith in Jesus Christ.

Our Father in Heaven, Who is merciful, gave us a Way out of "no way."

I LOVE THIS!

God Almighty sent Jesus Christ His One and Only Son, the Messiah to save us[8].

In Hebrews 1:1-4, the Bible says:

> "In the past God spoke to our ancestors through the prophets at many times and in various ways, but in these last days He has spoken to us by His Son, whom He appointed heir of all things, and through whom also He made the universe. The Son is the radiance of God's glory and the exact representation of His being, sustaining all things by His powerful word. After He had provided purification for sins, He sat down at the right hand of the Majesty in heaven. So He became as much superior to the angels as the name He has inherited is superior to theirs."

In John 14:1, Jesus tells us, "Do not let your hearts be troubled. You believe in God; believe also in me."

Remember, in Isaiah 59:1-2, the Lord said through the prophet Isaiah, "Surely the arm of the Lord is not too short to save, nor His ear too dull to hear. But your iniquities [sin] have separated you from your God; your sins have hidden His face from you, so that He will not hear."

Sin is what separates us from God, but it is by faith and faith alone in Jesus Christ that we are redeemed by the precious blood of God's Son.

In Hebrews 9:22, the Bible says, "In fact, the Law requires that nearly everything be cleansed with blood, and without the shedding of blood there is no forgiveness."

Our Lord Jesus shed His precious blood as he suffered, nailed to a cross, for you and me, for the sins of the world. Lord Jesus paid the ultimate price that no one else could pay.

In Isaiah 53:4-7, brother Isaiah prophesized:

>"Surely He took up our pain
>
>and bore our suffering,
>
>yet we considered Him punished by God,
>
>stricken by Him, and afflicted.
>
>But He was pierced for our transgressions,
>
>He was crushed for our iniquities;
>
>the punishment that brought us peace was on Him,
>
>and by His wounds we are healed.
>
>We all, like sheep, have gone astray,
>
>each of us has turned to our own way;
>
>and the Lord has laid on Him
>
>the iniquity of us all.
>
>He was oppressed and afflicted,
>
>yet He did not open His mouth;
>
>He was led like a lamb to the slaughter,

and as a sheep before its shearers is silent,

so He did not open His mouth."

In Matthew 16:21, as Jesus prepares his disciples for His upcoming sacrifice, brother Matthew states:

"From that time on Jesus began to explain to His disciples that He must go to Jerusalem and suffer many things at the hands of the elders, the chief priests and the teachers of the law, and that He must be killed and on the third day be raised to life."

In Romans 3:23-26, brother Paul says:

" ... for all have sinned and fall short of the glory of God, and all are justified freely by His grace through the redemption that came by Christ Jesus. God presented Christ as a sacrifice of atonement, through the shedding of His blood—to be received by faith. He did this to demonstrate His righteousness, because in His forbearance He had left the sins committed beforehand unpunished—He did it to demonstrate His righteousness at the present time, so as to be just and the one who justifies those who have faith in Jesus."

AMEN!

In Romans 4:25 brother Paul says, "He [Jesus Christ] was delivered over to death for our sins and was raised to life for our justification."

And again, in Romans 5:6-8, brother Paul states:

"You see, just at the right time, when we were still powerless, Christ died for the ungodly. Very rarely will anyone die for a righteous person, though for a good person someone might possibly dare to die. But God demonstrates His own love for us in this: While we were still sinners, Christ died for us."

Later, in Romans 8:3-4, brother Paul further explains:

"For what the Law was powerless to do because it was weakened by the flesh, God did by sending His Own Son in the likeness of sinful flesh to be a sin offering. And so He condemned sin in the flesh, in order that the righteous requirement of the Law might be fully met in us, who do not live according to the flesh but according to the Spirit."

In Ephesians 2:1-10, brother Paul writes:

"As for you, you were dead in your transgressions and sins, in which you used to live when you followed the ways of this world and of the ruler of the kingdom of the air, the spirit [Satan] who is now at work in those who are disobedient. All of us also lived among them at one time, gratifying the cravings of our flesh and following its desires and thoughts. Like the rest, we were by nature deserving of wrath. But because of His great love for us, God, who is rich in mercy, made us alive with Christ even when we were dead in transgressions—it is by grace you have been saved. And God raised us up with Christ and seated us with Him in the heavenly realms in Christ Jesus, in order that in the coming ages He might show the incomparable riches of His grace, expressed in His kindness to us in Christ Jesus. For it is by grace you have been saved, through faith—and this is not from yourselves, it is the gift of God— not by works, so that no one can boast. For we are God's handiwork, created in Christ Jesus to do good works, which God prepared in advance for us to do."

Nothing we say or do—other than accepting Jesus as our Lord and Savior—will take away our sins.

Reconciliation is through Christ and Christ alone. AMEN!

In 2 Corinthians 5:18-21, brother Paul writes:

"All this is from God, who reconciled us to Himself through Christ and gave us the ministry of reconciliation: That God was reconciling the world to Himself in Christ, not counting people's sins against them. And He has committed to us the message of reconciliation. We are therefore Christ's ambassadors, as though God were making His appeal through us. We implore you on Christ's behalf: Be reconciled to God. God made Him who had no sin to be sin for us, so that in Him we might become the righteousness of God."

As brother John says in 1 John 2:1-2:

"My dear children, I write this to you so that you will not sin. But if anybody does sin, we have an Advocate with the Father—Jesus Christ, the Righteous One. He is the atoning sacrifice for our sins, and not only for ours but also for the sins of the whole world."

PRAISE THE LORD!

And as the Bible says in John 3:16, "God so loved the world that He sent His One and Only Son Jesus Christ, that whoever believes in Him shall not perish but have eternal life."

Thank you, Jesus Christ, my Lord and Savior; my God and Friend!

Chapter 2
Taught by God

𝓘 am a young 28-year-old Black man as I write this. It is currently April 17, 2022, 8:29 p.m.

I have not been to school to learn about God.

I did not take ten years of religion classes to learn about God.

I have no scholarship from college.

I come from the neighborhood.

I earned my G.E.D. when I was seventeen, but besides that, I do not have much education from school to call myself well-learned. I am an average person; there is nothing special about me except my Lord Jesus Christ, Who saved me and turned my life around, and teaches me daily about God my Father through the Holy Spirit.

No man has taught me anything I know about God.

All my learning is directly from the Holy Spirit, through Whom the Lord Jesus speaks to me, sent by God Almighty Himself.

I find this truly amazing!

In Jeremiah 31:33-34, the Lord God said to brother Jeremiah:

"'This is the covenant I will make with the people of Israel

after that time,' declares the Lord.

'I will put my law in their minds

and write it on their hearts.

I will be their God,

and they will be my people.

No longer will they teach their neighbor,

or say to one another, "Know the Lord,"

because they will all know me,

from the least of them to the greatest,'

declares the Lord.

'For I will forgive their wickedness

and will remember their sins no more.'"

In Isaiah 54:13-14, the Lord God told brother Isaiah:

"All your children will be taught by the Lord,

and great will be their peace.

In righteousness you will be established:

Tyranny will be far from you;

you will have nothing to fear.

Terror will be far removed;

it will not come near you."

In Matthew 23:8 and 23:10, Lord Jesus said, " ... you are not to be called 'Rabbi,' for you have One Teacher, and you are all brothers. ... Nor are you to be called instructors, for you have One Instructor, the Messiah."

One thing I like to ask people is, "Where and from whom did you first learn about God?"

Nine times out of ten they will say someone told them about God.

There are plenty of schools that teach about God, but—sadly—in these schools there are many people who still have no clue about Who God Almighty truly is.

There are many people who grow up in a family with a religious background. A lot of people have a mother or father, sister or brother who says they are Christian. They could be Baptist, Jehovah's Witness, Methodist, Mormon, Episcopalian, Lutheran, Roman Catholic, or another sect of Christianity. Or they may be Jewish, Muslim, Hindu, Buddhist, or any number of other religions.

Here in the United States, it is easy for me or anyone to learn about religion on our own, but we could never really learn everything about God Almighty on our own.

I can try to come up with my own understanding of Who I think He is. I can pick up a book, access the Internet, or go anywhere on Earth to learn about religion on my own. I could study about God—many do! I can read the Bible 1,000 times and know every word from the front to the back, yet still not know anything about God Almighty.

Many call themselves teachers of God, yet they themselves still need to be taught about God Almighty. Many people cannot understand themselves, cannot explain why they act a certain way, yet claim they have God Almighty fully understood and can explain why God acts a certain way.

I highly doubt that. I cannot and will never be able to fully understand God Almighty, my Father. His knowledge surpasses mine a billion to one! As Isaiah 55:8-9 states:

> "For My thoughts are not your thoughts,
>
> neither are your ways My ways,"
>
> declares the Lord.
>
> "As the heavens are higher than the earth,
>
> so are My ways higher than your ways
>
> and My thoughts than your thoughts."

You see, I can try to teach somebody about God until I'm blue in the face. I have had many people try to talk to me about God when I was younger. They would have been better off talking to a wall. I have eyes that can see, but I was blind as a bat to God Almighty at one point in time. I have ears that can hear, but I was deaf to God's Word. I had an idea about God through others, but at one time I did not even want anything to do with Jesus Christ. At one point in time I did not believe in Jesus Christ.

But thank You, God; thank You, Jesus! Bless God Almighty, Who sent His One and Only Son anyway to save me and my life, even though I thought my life was worthless.

I didn't want anything to do with Jesus Christ because of the way I was living. I knew about God a little bit, but I was stuck in living, trusting in money. Oh, I believed enough about God at that time to know that God and the love of money do not mix. At that time, however, I felt like I had no choice. I thought I needed to focus on making money more than going to church.

But in my heart, I always felt like I was missing something, though I could never explain it.

I grew up in a family who knew about God and went to church, but that did not make a lot of sense to me. I really thought my family were just some "Jesus freaks," except for my great-grandmother. I knew there was something special about my great-grandmother, something different from anyone else I have known. I could see it clearly, but I did not understand it. She was serious about Jesus Christ and it showed in the way she lived. She held fast to Jesus like a wife would a husband, faithfully. She always talked about the Holy Ghost, and at times, it tripped me out. I did not know Who the Holy Ghost was, but I could see clearly my great-grandmother had something about her that was different from the rest of the people I knew. She just kept talking about Jesus, about the Holy Ghost, but I never understood her.

I remember some other people tried to talk to me about God and Jesus Christ but it didn't make much sense. One day, however, I came home and found a Bible on the table. I had been having a dreadful day. I picked up the Bible and just flipped through the pages when the name Jeremiah stood out to me, and I just started reading. It surprised me I could totally relate to everything Jeremiah had going on around him: wickedness, faithlessness, betrayal, persecution, ridicule.

In Psalms 107:20, the Bible says, "He sent His Word and healed them; He rescued them from the grave."

I tell you the truth: something led me to that Bible on the table. I was seventeen.

Something led me to pick up that Bible, and it was the Holy Spirit. Thank you, Jesus!

In Romans 8:14, brother Paul says, "For those who are led by the Spirit of God are the children of God."

Thank you, Jesus!

This was the first time the Bible spoke out to me. The words I read went straight into my heart. I could not explain the feeling, but I loved it.

In Jeremiah 15:16, brother Jeremiah states, "When Your words came, I ate them; they were my joy and my heart's delight, for I bear Your Name, Lord God Almighty."

Bless God Almighty for sending His Word, for revealing His Word to me. I could not see it on my own with my own eyes, even though it is written down in black and white. But God Almighty opened my eyes and my heart. He revealed Himself to me through reading His Word.

In 1 Samuel 3:21, the Bible says, "The Lord continued to appear at Shiloh, and there He revealed Himself to Samuel through His Word."

You see, there is a complete difference when you are learning from God Almighty versus learning about God from a school, on the Internet, from a book, or from a person. There is no comparison. God Almighty uses people like me to help teach people the Way, the Truth, and the Life, but unless God Almighty Himself shines His light on my words, then they remain hidden. Only God can shine the light, which makes the seeds grow that we plant.

Jesus Christ is the only One Who unfolds the Truth to make it clear.

I can tell you about the Truth, but it is only God Almighty Who allows you to understand it. Without Him being involved, you cannot understand it.

It is the Holy Spirit of God who teaches you the Truth. Without the Holy Spirit being involved, you cannot understand the Truth.

Without God Almighty putting the pieces of the puzzle together that He Himself created, it is impossible to learn everything you need to learn about Him. As Psalms 119:130 says, "The unfolding of Your words gives Light; it gives understanding to the simple."

You see, it is only when Jesus unfolds the Words of Truth and God Himself shines His light that I can understand what the Holy Spirit teaches me.

One might ask me:

How does God Almighty accomplish this?

How does He open my eyes?

How does He lead me to Jesus Christ?

How does He reveal His Word to me?

How does God carry out His acts?

In Zechariah 4:6, the Lord said, " ... This is the Word of the Lord to Zerubbabel: 'Not by might nor by power, but by My Spirit,' says the Lord Almighty." Amen! The Lord does all of this by His Holy Spirit.

It is very special—a very good thing—to grow up under a man or woman of God who tries to instruct you in life. That is a blessing to have, and it is highly beneficial to those who listen. But the best way—the only way—to truly learn about God Almighty is for the Holy Spirit to teach you, as the

Lord said in Isaiah 54:13 and repeated by Jesus in John 6:45: "All your children will be taught by God." There is no other way for us to understand Him.

I have had someone say to me, "Davante, you have helped show me many things about God I did not know." In response I said, "Thank you, but all glory, honor, and praise goes to my Father, God Almighty, Who sent Jesus Christ, Who loved me enough to die on a cross and give me the gift of the Holy Spirit."

The Holy Spirit teaches me each and every day about my Lord and Savior, Jesus Christ.

The Holy Spirit teaches me about God Almighty, my Father in Heaven.

The Holy Spirit teaches me daily as I teach others. I receive no credit. All glory, honor, and praise goes to Him.

Truly, without the Holy Spirit teaching me, I would never be able to learn about Him.

I can develop my own thoughts about God; many people do just that.

But it is not going to make much sense once the limit of human understanding is exceeded. You see, it is impossible to understand God Almighty 100%. Even I, with all that the Holy Spirit teaches me, will never be able to understand God 100%. His knowledge surpasses mine and all others'. He is the only One worthy of praise, honor, and glory.

If I could understand God Almighty 100%, then He would not *be* God Almighty at all. I only know what I know because of the Holy Spirit, and what God has revealed to me through Him. I remember I had my own ideas about God at one time, but when God began teaching me through the Holy Spirit, it was like no other education.

God Almighty uses people like me who have the Holy Spirit within to instruct others about God, to plant the seeds of God's Word in people's hearts, but it is only God Himself Who does the true teaching through the Holy Spirit. God Almighty, Who sent His One and Only Son, Jesus Christ, Who operates through the Holy Spirit to unfold the Truth upon which God shines His glorious Light in order for you and me to see, hear, and understand His Truth.

In John 8:12, Lord Jesus says, " ... I am the Light of the world. Whoever follows Me will never walk in darkness. but will have the Light of life."

Without God Almighty, nothing makes sense. Without the Light of God shining on Jesus unfolding the Truth through the Holy Spirit, God's Word is only just a story or a fairy tale; some might even call it a lie. Without the Light of God, no one would be able to understand. As brother Paul says in 1 Corinthians 2:14, "The person without the Spirit does not accept the things that come from the Spirit of God but considers them foolishness, and cannot understand them because they are discerned only through the Spirit."

AMEN!

It all starts with God's Word. He sent His Word to teach us Truth, to heal us, to bring us out of the darkness into the Light. Psalms 107:20 states, "He sent out His Word and healed them: He rescued them from the grave." Likewise, as Paul says in 1 Timothy 3:16-17:

"All Scripture is God-breathed and is useful for teaching, rebuking, correcting and training in righteousness, so that the servant of God may be thoroughly equipped for every good work."

In John 1:1-5, 12, and 14, John says:

"In the beginning was the Word, and the Word was with God, and the Word was God. He was with God in the beginning. Through Him all things were made; without Him nothing was made that has been made. In Him was life, and that life was the Light of all mankind. The Light shines in the darkness, and the darkness has not overcome it … to all who did receive Him, to those who believed in His name, He gave the right to become children of God … The Word became flesh and made His dwelling among us. We have seen His glory, the glory of the One and Only Son, Who came from the Father, full of grace and truth."

AMEN!

In John 14:15-18, the Lord Jesus said:

"If you love Me, keep My commands. And I will ask the Father, and He will give you another Advocate to help you and be with you forever—the Spirit of Truth. The world cannot accept Him, because it neither sees Him nor knows Him. But you know Him, for He lives with you and will be in you. I will not leave you as orphans; I will come to you."

In John 15:5-8, the Lord Jesus said:

"I am the vine; you are the branches. If you remain in Me and I in you, you will bear much fruit; apart from Me you can do nothing. If you do not remain in Me, you are like a branch that is thrown away and withers; such branches are picked up, thrown into the fire and burned. If you remain in Me and My words remain in you, ask whatever you wish, and it will be done for you. This is to My Father's glory, that you bear much fruit, showing yourselves to be My disciples."

And in John 16:7-15, the Lord Jesus said:

"But very truly I tell you, it is for your good that I am going away. Unless I go away, the Advocate will not come to you; but if I go, I will send Him to you. When He comes, He will prove the world to be in the wrong about sin and righteousness and judgment: about sin, because people do not believe in Me; about righteousness, because I am going to the Father, where you can see Me no longer; and about judgment, because the Prince of this world now stands condemned.

"I have much more to say to you, more than you can now bear. But when He, the Spirit of Truth, comes, He will guide you into all the truth. He will not speak on His own; He will speak only what He hears, and He will tell you what is yet to come. He will glorify Me because it is from Me that He will receive what He will make known to you. All that belongs to the Father is Mine. That is why I said the Spirit will receive from Me what He will make known to you."

Jesus tells us in John 6:44-45:

"No one can come to Me unless the Father Who sent Me draws them, and I will raise them up at the last day. It is written in the

Prophets: 'They will all be taught by God.' Everyone who has heard the Father and learned from Him comes to Me."

Last, but certainly not least, in John 14:6, Jesus answers Thomas's question on how the disciples will know the way to the Lord's destination: "I am the Way and the Truth and the Life. No one comes to the Father except through Me. If you really know Me, you will know My Father as well. From now on, you do know Him and have seen Him."

I cannot go to Jesus Christ on my own unless the Father Who sent Jesus draws me there by the Holy Spirit.

I cannot come to God my Father on my own. Only through Jesus Christ am I allowed access to my Father, and this is done by the Holy Spirit.

It is the Holy Spirit Who leads us to God's Word, Jesus Christ Himself, Who then one day, the day of His coming, will lead us home to our Father in Heaven.

AMEN!

Chapter 3
The Lord Will Teach Us

The Lord our God, Jesus Christ Himself, will teach us His Ways through the Holy Spirit.

Our Father in Heaven will teach us His Ways through the Holy Spirit.

All we have to do is turn to Jesus earnestly with all our heart, soul, and mind. If we do that, the Bible says He will pour out His Spirit upon us. All we have to do is ask Jesus Christ to help us, and then just be patient.

In Psalms 25:4-6, brother David prays:

> "Show me Your Ways, Lord,
>
> teach me Your paths.
>
> Guide me in Your truth and teach me,
>
> for You are God my Savior,
>
> and my hope is in You all day long.
>
> Remember, Lord, Your great mercy and love,
>
> for they are from of old."

David further prays in Psalms 86:11:

"Teach me Your Way, Lord,

that I may rely on Your faithfulness;

give me an undivided heart,

that I may fear Your Name."

In Proverbs 1:27, the Lord said through Solomon, David's son:

"Repent at My rebuke!

Then I will pour out My Spirit onto you;

I will make known to you My teachings."

Brother Moses said in Deuteronomy 30:1-6:

"When all these blessings and curses I have set before you come on you and you take them to heart wherever the Lord your God disperses you among the nations, and when you and your children return to the Lord your God and obey Him with all your heart and with all your soul according to everything I command you today, then the Lord your God will restore your fortunes and have compassion on you and gather you again from all the nations where He scattered you. Even if you have been banished to the most distant land under the heavens, from there the Lord your God will gather you and bring you back. He will bring you to the land that belonged to your ancestors, and you will take possession of it. He will make you more prosperous and numerous than your ancestors. The Lord your God will circumcise your hearts and the hearts of your descendants, so that you may love Him with all your heart and with all your soul, and live."

And in Deuteronomy 30:19-20, brother Moses advised the Israelites:

"This day I call the heavens and the earth as witnesses against you that I have set before you life and death, blessings and curses. Now choose life, so that you and your children may live and that you may love the Lord your God, listen to His voice, and hold fast to Him. For the Lord is your life, and He will give you many years in the land He swore to give to your fathers, Abraham, Isaac and Jacob."

The Bible says in Isaiah 2:1-5:

"This is what Isaiah son of Amoz saw concerning Judah and Jerusalem:

In the last days

the mountain of the Lord's temple will be established

as the highest of the mountains;

it will be exalted above the hills,

and all nations will stream to it.

Many peoples will come and say,

'Come, let us go up to the mountain of the Lord,

to the temple of the God of Jacob.

He will teach us His ways,

so that we may walk in His paths.'

The law will go out from Zion,

the word of the Lord from Jerusalem.

He will judge between the nations

and will settle disputes for many peoples.

They will beat their swords into plowshares

and their spears into pruning hooks.

Nation will not take up sword against nation,

nor will they train for war anymore.

Come, descendants of Jacob,

let us walk in the Light of the Lord."

They were ready to walk in the Light of the Lord. They were ready to walk in God's Word.

In Psalms 119:105, the Bible says, "Your Word is a lamp for my feet, a Light on my path."

In John 8:12, Lord Jesus said, "I am the Light of the world. Whoever follows Me will never walk in darkness, but will have the Light of life." AMEN!

And in John 15:7, Lord Jesus said, "If you remain in Me and My words remain in you, ask whatever you wish, and it will be done for you."

AMEN! It all starts with God's Word.

In John 1:1-5, 12, and 14, John says:

"In the beginning was the Word, and the Word was with God, and the Word was God. He was with God in the beginning. Through Him all things were made; without Him nothing was made that has been made. In Him was life, and that life was the Light of all mankind. The Light shines in the darkness, and the darkness has not overcome it ... to all who did receive Him, to those who believed in His name, He gave the right to become children of God ... The Word became flesh and made His dwelling among us. We have seen His glory, the glory of the One and Only Son, Who came from the Father, full of grace and truth."

Brother Isaiah said in Isaiah 55:6-7:

"Seek the Lord while He may be found;

call on Him while He is near.

Let the wicked forsake their ways

and the unrighteous their thoughts.

Let them turn to the Lord, and He will have mercy on them,

and to our God, for He will freely pardon."

And in Revelation 22:12-16, Jesus Christ says:

"Look, I am coming soon! My reward is with me, and I will give to each person according to what they have done. I am the Alpha and the Omega, the First and the Last, the Beginning and the End.

"Blessed are those who wash their robes, that they may have the right to the tree of life and may go through the gates into the city. Outside are the dogs, those who practice magic arts, the sexually immoral, the murderers, the idolaters and everyone who loves and practices falsehood.

"I, Jesus, have sent my angel to give you this testimony for the churches. I am the Root and the Offspring of David, and the bright Morning Star."

AMEN!

In Psalms 90:12 and 17, brother Moses prayed:

"Teach us to number our days,

that we may gain a heart of wisdom ...

May the favor of the Lord our God rest on us;

establish the work of our hands for us—

yes, establish the work of our hands."

AMEN! We need to cherish the time we have and focus our energy—our work—on what pleases God, not ourselves.

Keep looking towards God Almighty our Father, towards our Lord Jesus Christ His One and Only Son, and towards the Holy Spirit for direction. Keep trusting in the Lord Jesus Christ with all your heart and lean not on your own understanding, for He will direct your path. AMEN!

Chapter 4
How Important is the Holy Spirit?

I would like to ask a question of everyone. How important is the Holy Spirit? The Holy Spirit is *very* important.

Listen carefully!

In 1 John 5:7 (KJV) brother John says, "For there are Three that bear record in Heaven, the Father, the Word, and the Holy Ghost [Spirit]: and these Three are One." AMEN!

In Genesis 1:1-2, the Bible says, "In the beginning God created the heavens and the earth. Now the earth was formless and empty, darkness was over the surface of the deep, and the Spirit of God was hovering over the waters."

The Holy Spirit was there *from the beginning*, hovering over the waters.

Brother John says in John 1:1-5 and 14:

> In the beginning was the Word, and the Word was with God, and the Word was God. He was with God in the beginning. Through Him all things were made; without Him nothing was made that has

been made. In Him was Life, and that Life was the Light of all mankind. The Light shines in the darkness, and the darkness has not overcome it ... The Word became flesh and made His dwelling among us. We have seen His glory, the glory of the One and Only Son, Who came from the Father, full of grace and truth."

How important is the Holy Spirit? In Jeremiah 31:33, the Bible says:

"This is the covenant I will make with the people of Israel

after that time," declares the Lord.

"I will put My Law in their minds

and write it on their hearts.

I will be their God,

and they will be My people."

How does the Lord put His Law in our minds and write it on our hearts? This is done by the Holy Spirit.

In Proverbs 1:23 (NKJV), the Lord said:

"Turn at My rebuke;

Surely I will pour out My Spirit on you.

I will make My Words known to you."

The Lord wants us to repent and turn to Him! AMEN!

If we accept God's Word, He will pour out His Spirit and make His Words known to us.

If we follow God's Word, then in a manner of speaking, we are also following the Spirit of God's Commandments; we are doing what the Spirit of God says to our heart and mind.

And when we follow God's Word, then in a manner of speaking, we are also following Jesus Christ through the Holy Spirit, through God's Commandments.

We are led by God's Spirit through God's Word.

Brother Paul says in Romans 8:5, "Those who live according to the flesh have their minds set on what the flesh desires; but those who live in accordance with the Spirit have their minds set on what the Spirit desires."

Paul continues in Romans 8:26-27:

> "In the same way, the Spirit helps us in our weakness. We do not know what we ought to pray for, but the Spirit Himself intercedes for us through wordless groans. And he who searches our hearts knows the mind of the Spirit, because the Spirit intercedes for God's people in accordance with the will of God."

Thank you, Father; thank you, Lord Jesus; and thank you, sweet Holy Spirit!

How important is the Holy Spirit?

Lord Jesus tells a Samaritan woman in John 4:24, "God is Spirit, and His worshipers must worship in the Spirit and in truth."

In John 4:44-45, on the day after Jesus fed a crowd of about 5,000 men, the Lord answered the people grumbling about His statement that He was the Bread that came down from Heaven:

> "No one can come to Me unless the Father Who sent Me draws them, and I will raise them up at the last day. It is written in the

Prophets: 'They will all be taught by God.' Everyone who has heard the Father and learned from Him comes to Me."

And in John 6:63, Lord Jesus tells His disciples, "The Spirit gives Life; the flesh counts for nothing. The words I have spoken to you—they are full of the Spirit and Life."

How important is the Holy Spirit?

The Holy Spirit gives Life, and this Life is found in Jesus Christ!

In John 7:37-39, when the disciples and Lord Jesus are at the Festival of the Tabernacle, brother John records:

> "On the last and greatest day of the festival, Jesus stood and said in a loud voice, 'Let anyone who is thirsty come to Me and drink. Whoever believes in Me, as Scripture has said, rivers of living water will flow from within them.' By this He meant the Spirit, Whom those who believed in Him were later to receive. Up to that time the Spirit had not been given, since Jesus had not yet been glorified."

Lord Jesus says to come to Him and believe in Him, and the Holy Spirit will flow from within us!

In John 14:15-17, Lord Jesus promises His disciples—and us—the Holy Spirit will come:

> "If you love Me, keep My commands. And I will ask the Father, and He will give you another Advocate to help you and be with you forever—the Spirit of Truth. The world cannot accept Him, because it neither sees Him nor knows Him. But you know Him, for He lives with you and will be in you."

HOW IMPORTANT IS THE HOLY SPIRIT?

In John 15:26-27, Lord Jesus further explains:

> "When the Advocate comes, Whom I will send to you from the Father—the Spirit of Truth Who goes out from the Father—He will testify about Me. And you also must testify, for you have been with Me from the beginning."

And in John 16:7-16, Lord Jesus continues to prepare His disciples for His pending death:

> " ... very truly I tell you, it is for your good that I am going away. Unless I go away, the Advocate will not come to you; but if I go, I will send Him to you. When He comes, He will prove the world to be in the wrong about sin and righteousness and judgment: about sin, because people do not believe in Me; about righteousness, because I am going to the Father, where you can see Me no longer; and about judgment, because the prince of this world [Satan] now stands condemned.

> "I have much more to say to you, more than you can now bear. But when He, the Spirit of Truth, comes, He will guide you into all the Truth. He will not speak on His own; He will speak only what He hears, and He will tell you what is yet to come. He will glorify Me because it is from Me that He will receive what He will make known to you. All that belongs to the Father is Mine. That is why I said the Spirit will receive from Me what He will make known to you."

AMEN!

How important is the Holy Spirit?

The Holy Spirit is *very* important! He is required because without Him we cannot understand our Father God Almighty or His Son Lord Jesus Christ. Without the Holy Spirit, nothing makes sense. You cannot even accept the things that come from God because they are spiritually discerned through the Holy Spirit.

In 1 Corinthians 2:12-14, brother Paul writes:

> "What we have received is not the spirit of the world, but the Spirit who is from God, so that we may understand what God has freely given us. This is what we speak, not in words taught us by human wisdom but in words taught by the Spirit, explaining spiritual realities with Spirit-taught words. The person without the Spirit does not accept the things that come from the Spirit of God but considers them foolishness, and cannot understand them because they are discerned only through the Spirit."

In Galatians 5:16, brother Paul writes, "So I say, walk by the Spirit, and you will not gratify the desires of the flesh."

Brother Paul continues in Galatians 5:22-23:

> " ... the fruit of the Spirit is love, joy, peace, forbearance [mercy], kindness, goodness, faithfulness, gentleness, and self-control. Against such things there is no law."

And in Zechariah 4:6, brother Zechariah speaks of an angel's revelation to him on the rebuilding of the Temple: "So he said to me, 'This is the Word of the Lord to Zerubbabel: "Not by might nor by power, but by My Spirit," says the Lord Almighty.'"

So, how important is the Holy Spirit?

HOW IMPORTANT IS THE HOLY SPIRIT?

The Holy Spirit is VERY important, for He teaches us, leads us, prays for us, and guides us through the Word of God, which leads to Jesus Christ, Who is the Living Word of God.

AMEN!

Chapter 5

Daily Readings for Your Mind, Heart, and Spirit

Many days I have been upset.

Many days I need to watch my mouth. I can go off sometimes and "speak my mind."

I'm sure you know what I mean.

Sometimes, however, Solomon's words from Proverbs 15:1 can stop me from being mean and rude: "A gentle answer turns away wrath, but a harsh word stirs up anger." AMEN! Forgive me, Lord Jesus!

If I could go back and think before I said some things to people, the outcomes would have been completely different. But most often, as the Bible says in Proverbs 16:18, "Pride goes before destruction, a haughty spirit before a fall."

There have been many times when I was not able to be gentle or kind because my pride was in the way. But once pride has been removed, then I can be humble.

In Matthew 23:12, Lord Jesus said, " ... those who exalt themselves will be humbled, and those who humble themselves will be exalted." AMEN!

You see, quite often in each and every battle on this battlefield called Earth, I can cause a war or prevent a war with the words from my mouth.

An agreement, a discussion, or doing something right can prevent war. But, an argument, a fight, or a wrong can start a war. It does not take much for a fire to start if there is gasoline already on the floor. All you need is a spark and everything goes up in smoke!

Listen, friends: we have to put our pride to the side no matter how much wrong we have done to others or others have done to us! Fire plus fire is a bigger fire. Fire must be put out with water, or at the very least, you need to let it die down and burn out. Do not keep adding more fuel!

In James 1:19-22, brother James said:

> "My dear brothers and sisters, take note of this: Everyone should be quick to listen, slow to speak, and slow to become angry, because human anger does not produce the righteousness that God desires. Therefore, get rid of all moral filth and the evil that is so prevalent and humbly accept the word planted in you, which can save you.
>
> "Do not merely listen to the Word, and so deceive yourselves. Do what it says!"

AMEN!

One day, after the Pharisees and teachers of the law questioned Lord Jesus about why His disciples broke tradition by not washing their hands before eating, and the disciples claimed the Pharisees had been insulted by the Lord's reply, Jesus said to them in Matthew 15:16-20:

> "Are you still so dull? ... Don't you see that whatever enters the mouth goes into the stomach and then out of the body? But the things that come out of a person's mouth come from the heart, and these defile them. For out of the heart come evil thoughts—murder, adultery, sexual immorality, theft, false testimony, slander. These are what defile a person; but eating with unwashed hands does not defile them."

Defile means to ruin, poison, pollute, corrupt, or destroy.

So if I say mean, hateful, hurtful words to someone, or cause another person to do the same thing, I defile myself.

Pride, murder, slander, lies, theft, immorality, and the like are SINS. I can choose to be wicked, but being wicked is not the Way. It leads to sin and sin leads to death.

It is a cold, evil, hateful, murderous, sinful, and dark world in which we live. But praise God Almighty Who sent His Son Jesus Christ so that all who believe in Him shall not die and instead have eternal life. Lord Jesus was sent to die on a cross for my sins, for your sins, and for the sins of the whole world so we who believe in Him will have eternal life. Thank You, Jesus!

In 1 John 2:1-2, brother John writes:

> "My dear children, I write this to you so that you will not sin. But if anybody does sin, we have an advocate with the Father—Jesus Christ, the Righteous One. He is the atoning sacrifice for our sins, and not only for ours but also for the sins of the whole world."

You see, nobody wins in a life of sin.

Nobody wins when controlled by sin, or paying sin back with sin.

But there is a Way that leads to peace—Jesus Christ is the Way!

It's sad to say that today it seems a human being's life means nothing to a lot of people, but that is the world in which we live. People kill other people every day, and with no remorse whatsoever! It's like, if you do something to me, then I'm going to do something to you to get even; after all, it's an eye for eye, right? Or, I might decide to do you more harm than you did me, just to make sure you get my "message." It seems nowadays that is basically how we are living.

Well, nobody wins like that!

The Lord God said in Exodus 20:13, "You shall not murder."

In Romans 12:17-19, brother Paul writes:

> "Do not repay anyone evil for evil. Be careful to do what is right in the eyes of everyone. If it is possible, as far as it depends on you, live at peace with everyone. Do not take revenge, my dear friends, but leave room for God's wrath, for it is written: 'It is Mine to avenge; I will repay, says the Lord.' On the contrary: If your enemy is hungry; if he is thirsty, give him something to drink. In doing this, you will heap burning coals on his head. Do not be overcome by evil, but overcome evil with good."

AMEN!

We live in a world where there is a whole lot of hate going on, along with jealousy, anger, and murder.

It all starts in your heart.

Before murder comes hate or anger for whatever reason. It does not matter whether you are right or wrong; the fact is, it is sin to repay back anything that has happened to you. Do not get even!

It all starts in your heart.

In Matthew 5:21-22, Lord Jesus speaks to the crowd on the Mount of Beatitudes, saying:

> "You have heard that it was said to the people long ago, 'You shall not murder, and anyone who murders will be subject to judgment.' But I tell you that anyone who is angry with a brother or sister will be subject to judgment. Again, anyone who says to a brother or sister, '*Raca*,' [worthless] is answerable to the court. And anyone who says, 'You fool!' will be in danger of the fire of hell."

Being angry with someone in your heart is just as bad as murdering someone. Sin is sin. To hate a brother or sister in your heart is no less sinful than if you murder them.

In 1 John 3:15, brother John said, "Anyone who hates a brother or sister is a murderer, and you know that no murderer has eternal life residing in him." AMEN!

It all starts in your heart: murder comes from anger and hate in your heart.

Sin is sin! You cannot justify sin!

There are plenty of good reasons to get mad at someone, but in your anger, DO NOT SIN.

In Ephesians 4:26-27, brother Paul writes, "In your anger do not sin: Do not let the sun go down while you are still angry, and do not give the devil a foothold."

Anger is normal, but letting it take over you leads to sin. A person might say, "My girlfriend cheated on me, so now I hate her and whoever she is with. What should I do? Should I adopt the mindset and cheat on others like I have been cheated on?"

NO! Nobody wins in a life of sin.

Listen, I have been shot by someone with a gun. Should I go out and shoot them back? After all, I have a good reason to want to, and I'm not afraid. Should I get even, or shoot other people because I've been shot?

NO! Nobody wins in a life of sin.

I have been beaten, stolen from, lied to, and talked about. I had my name dragged all up and down the mud. Should I get even and start beating other folk, stealing, lying, and talking about people? Should I drag their names up and down the mud? I can do it way better than they did me. Getting even is so easy!

Nevertheless, NOBODY WINS IN A LIFE OF SIN!

As Paul tells the Romans in Romans 12:21, "Do not be overcome by evil, but overcome evil with good." AMEN!

But we live in a pretty evil world, right? Tell me, what is good?

Great question.

In Matthew 19:17, when a young man asked the Lord what good thing he had to do in order to receive eternal life, Jesus replied, "Why do you ask Me about what is good? There is only One Who is good."

The One Who is good is God Almighty.

THIS is how we overcome the evil in this world:

WITH God Almighty,

BY God Almighty, and

THROUGH God's Word! AMEN!

Chapter 6
Love

Do you want to know from whom I receive the most hate? I'm sad to say this, but it is my own people most of the time.

Lord Jesus was sent to His own people, the Hebrews, yet His own did not receive Him. I feel that one hundred percent!

Yes, it is my own people I'm talking about—church people—so it is no wonder why a lot of people do not want anything to do with Jesus Christ, especially when they come across some people who claim to know Jesus and say they bear His Name yet do nothing to show it towards others.

Notice I said, "some people."

There are many other people whom I have come across, and they are the most kind-hearted, the sweetest people that will do anything for you out of the love they have for Jesus Christ. I thank God Almighty for this. These people claim to know God Almighty, Jesus Christ, and the Holy Spirit and demonstrate God's mercy, love, and grace to others. These folks give Him a good Name and inspire others to want to be like them: loving, kind, gentle, self-controlled, patient, and full of goodness. They accept God's Word, and they follow God's Word.

Yet there are some who give our Father God, our Lord Jesus, and the Holy Spirit a bad name.

Some people who claim to know Jesus Christ can be mean, have a bad attitude, and are judgmental about everything. They are true hypocrites. And Lord Jesus Himself calls them hypocrites in Matthew 24:13:

> "Woe to you, teachers of the law and Pharisees, you hypocrites! You shut the door of the kingdom of heaven in people's faces. You yourselves do not enter, nor will you let those enter who are trying to."

These people are supposed to be the children of the Most High God Almighty. They claim to know Who Jesus Christ is, and to have the Holy Spirit within themselves, and sadly, it is possible they do. Nevertheless, they can be nasty to people and judgmental; they can be fault-finders and grumblers, always ready to argue or fight, never knowing the way of peace.

Who wants to be around that? I know I sure don't!

I'm one of God's children as well, yet sometimes it is hard for me to be around these people. But God bless them, I still love them and I pray for them despite the fact they are some of the most stiff-necked, stubborn, and rebellious people I have ever come across. These folks do not represent God in a way that honors Him.

I can understand why people turn to drugs, sex, alcohol, or whatever else there is to escape life. Life is difficult. People will turn to drugs and other substances before they turn to God, sad to say, and I cannot blame them if the only "Christians" they have met are mean and judgmental. We are supposed to be God's people!

Look at how we act towards one another. As Lord Jesus said in Matthew 24:15:

> "Woe to you, teachers of the law and Pharisees, you hypocrites! You travel over land and sea to win a single convert, and when you have succeeded, you make them twice as much a child of hell as you are."

Do you think people will want anything to do with God when some of the flock represent Him so badly and everyone can see it? Where is the love?

At times, people see God's children behaving even worse than they do. Why would anyone want anything to do with Jesus Christ or the Holy Spirit when they see how some of us act and treat each other? The world sees and hears those who blaspheme the Name of God by their behavior, so why would they bother listening to someone who claims to follow God but demonstrates otherwise?

In Romans 2:-21-24, brother Paul writes:

> " ... you, then, who teach others, do you not teach yourself? You who preach against stealing, do you steal? You who say that people should not commit adultery, do you commit adultery? You who abhor idols, do you rob temples? You who boast in the law, do you dishonor God by breaking the law? As it is written: 'God's name is blasphemed among the Gentiles because of you.'"

That is so true! I write this specifically to and for God's children, my brothers and sisters who act like children of the world instead of as children of the Most High. I myself am one of God's children, and I am not perfect. I know I need help just like the rest of the world. I am still growing, but we can ALL do better! We really have to practice more of what we preach. You see, our actions and ways can make God our Father, Lord Jesus Christ, and the Holy Spirit look bad when we know for a fact how good God our Father, Lord Jesus Christ, and the Holy Spirit are to us. We ought to ACT like it!

LOVE is at the center of everything.

In 1 Peter 4:8, Peter writes, "Above all, love each other deeply, because love covers over a multitude of sins."

In John 3:16, brother John said, "For God so loved the world that He gave His One and Only Son, that whoever believes in Him shall not perish but have eternal life."

In Romans 5:6-8, brother Paul writes:

"You see, at just the right time, when we were still powerless, Christ died for the ungodly. Very rarely will anyone die for a righteous person, though for a good person someone might possibly dare to die. But God demonstrates His own love for us in this: While we were still sinners, Christ died for us."

In 1 John 3:16-18, brother John writes:

"This is how we know what love is: Jesus Christ laid down his life for us. And we ought to lay down our lives for our brothers and sisters. If anyone has material possessions and sees a brother or sister in need but has no pity on them, how can the love of God be in that person? Dear children, let us not love with words or speech but with actions and in truth."

In Romans 12:9-18, brother Paul writes:

"Love must be sincere. Hate what is evil; cling to what is good. Be devoted to one another in love. Honor one another above yourselves. Never be lacking in zeal, but keep your spiritual fervor, serving the Lord. Be joyful in hope, patient in affliction, faithful in prayer. Share with the Lord's people who are in need. Practice hospitality.

"Bless those who persecute you; bless and do not curse. Rejoice with those who rejoice; mourn with those who mourn. Live in harmony with one another. Do not be proud, but be willing to associate with people of low position. Do not be conceited.

"Do not repay anyone evil for evil. Be careful to do what is right in the eyes of everyone. If it is possible, as far as it depends on you, live at peace with everyone."

In Romans 13:8-10, brother Paul writes:

"Let no debt remain outstanding, except the continuing debt to love one another, for whoever loves others has fulfilled the law. The commandments, 'You shall not commit adultery,' 'You shall not murder,' 'You shall not steal,' 'You shall not covet,' and whatever other command there may be, are summed up in this one command: 'Love your neighbor as yourself.' Love does no harm to a neighbor. Therefore love is the fulfillment of the Law."

AMEN! Love is the fulfillment of the Law of God!

In Matthew 22:34-40, brother Matthew recorded:

> "Hearing that Jesus had silenced the Sadducees, the Pharisees got together. One of them, an expert in the law, tested him with this question: 'Teacher, which is the greatest commandment in the Law?'

> "Jesus replied: '"Love the Lord your God with all your heart and with all your soul and with all your mind." This is the first and greatest commandment. And the second is like it: "Love your neighbor as yourself." All the Law and the Prophets hang on these two commandments.'"

Love is indispensable: absolutely necessary, essential, key, vital, needed, required, all-important, life or death, high priority!

Brother Paul writes in 1 Corinthians 13:1-13:

> "If I speak in the tongues of men or of angels, but do not have love, I am only a resounding gong or a clanging cymbal. If I have the gift of prophecy and can fathom all mysteries and all knowledge, and if I have a faith that can move mountains, but do not have love, I am nothing. If I give all I possess to the poor and give over my body to hardship that I may boast, but do not have love, I gain nothing.

> "Love is patient, love is kind. It does not envy, it does not boast, it is not proud. It does not dishonor others, it is not self-seeking, it is not easily angered, it keeps no record of wrongs. Love does not delight in evil but rejoices with the truth. It always protects, always trusts, always hopes, always perseveres.

"Love never fails. But where there are prophecies, they will cease; where there are tongues, they will be stilled; where there is knowledge, it will pass away. For we know in part and we prophesy in part, but when completeness comes, what is in part disappears. When I was a child, I talked like a child, I thought like a child, I reasoned like a child. When I became a man, I put the ways of childhood behind me. For now we see only a reflection as in a mirror; then we shall see face to face. Now I know in part; then I shall know fully, even as I am fully known.

And now these three remain: faith, hope, and love. But the greatest of these is love."

Brother John writes in 1 John 4:7-12:

"Dear friends, let us love one another, for love comes from God. Everyone who loves has been born of God and knows God. Whoever does not love does not know God, because God is love. This is how God showed His love among us: He sent His One and Only Son into the world that we might live through Him. This is love: not that we loved God, but that He loved us and sent His Son as an atoning sacrifice for our sins. Dear friends, since God so loved us, we also ought to love one another. No one has ever seen God; but if we love one another, God lives in us and His love is made complete in us."

Brother John further says in 1 John 4:18-21:

"There is no fear in love. But perfect love drives out fear, because fear has to do with punishment. The one who fears is not made perfect in love.

"We love because He first loved us. Whoever claims to love God yet hates a brother or sister is a liar. For whoever does not love their brother and sister, whom they have seen, cannot love God, whom they have not seen. And He has given us this command: Anyone who loves God must also love their brother and sister."

In Luke 6:27-36, Jesus says to His disciples:

"But to you who are listening I say: Love your enemies, do good to those who hate you, bless those who curse you, pray for those who mistreat you. If someone slaps you on one cheek, turn to them the other also. If someone takes your coat, do not withhold your shirt from them. Give to everyone who asks you, and if anyone takes what belongs to you, do not demand it back. Do to others as you would have them do to you.

"If you love those who love you, what credit is that to you? Even sinners love those who love them. And if you do good to those who are good to you, what credit is that to you? Even sinners do that. And if you lend to those from whom you expect repayment, what credit is that to you? Even sinners lend to sinners, expecting to be repaid in full. But love your enemies, do good to them, and lend to them without expecting to get anything back. Then your reward will be great, and you will be children of the Most High, because He is kind to the ungrateful and wicked. Be merciful, just as your Father is merciful."

And in John 13:34-35, on the evening of His betrayal by Judas, Jesus commands His disciples, "A new command I give you: Love one another. As I have loved you, so you must love one another. By this everyone will know that you are My disciples, if you love one another."

With all of the things I have been through in my life, I remember at one point in time when I did not want anything to do with Jesus Christ. I was stuck in my ways, living a life of sin. I could not understand God. I did not have time for God! I used to ask if God was even real, and if He is, why didn't He help me? I wanted to know why a lot of bad things always happened to me, bad things I did not deserve? I used to feel like I was alienated from God.

In Colossians 1:21-23, brother Paul writes:

> "Once you were alienated from God and were enemies in your minds because of your evil behavior. But now He has reconciled you by Christ's physical body through death to present you holy in His sight, without blemish and free from accusation— if you continue in your faith, established and firm, and do not move from the hope held out in the gospel. This is the gospel that you heard and that has been proclaimed to every creature under heaven, and of which I, Paul, have become a servant."

I, too, was once an enemy to God, and I can admit it. I did not know Who Jesus Christ was at the time; my family did, but I did not. It used to make me so mad! I felt like Jesus didn't wany anything to do with me. In fact, I admit I used to hate the Name of Jesus!

Now, however, Jesus Christ is the Sweetest Name I know, my Closest Friend, my Lord and Savior! Back then, I felt dead on the inside to God. I had a lot of anger towards God. But thank God for His mercy—His grace—His love!

In Ephesians 2:1-10, brother Paul writes:

> "As for you, you were dead in your transgressions and sins, in which you used to live when you followed the ways of this world and of the ruler of the kingdom of the air, the spirit who is now at work in those who are disobedient. All of us also lived among them at one time, gratifying the cravings of our flesh and following its desires and thoughts. Like the rest, we were by nature deserving of wrath. But because of His great love for us, God, Who is rich in mercy, made us alive with Christ even when we were dead in transgressions—it is by grace you have been saved. And God raised us up with Christ and seated us with Him in the heavenly realms in Christ Jesus, in order that in the coming ages He might show the incomparable riches of His grace, expressed in His kindness to us in Christ Jesus. For it is by grace you have been saved, through faith—and this is not from yourselves, it is the gift of God—not by works, so that no one can boast. For we are God's handiwork, created in Christ Jesus to do good works, which God prepared in advance for us to do."

AMEN!

I remember when my spirit was overwhelmed. I did not have any hope. I did not choose God, but God Almighty in His mercy and His grace that is found in Jesus Christ, chose me! I was on the wrong road and not living right, down deep in sin, but the kindness of God, the mercy of God, the grace of God, and the LOVE of God is rich beyond measure! He sees beyond all of our faults and is able to wash us clean.

In Isaiah 1:18, the Lord said, " ... Though your sins are like scarlet, they shall be white as snow; though they are red as crimson, they shall be white as wool." AMEN!

In Titus 3:4-7, brother Paul writes:

> " ... when the kindness and love of God our Savior appeared, He saved us, not because of righteous things we had done, but because of His mercy. He saved us through the washing of rebirth and renewal by the Holy Spirit, Whom He poured out on us generously through Jesus Christ our Savior, so that, having been justified by His grace, we might become heirs having the hope of eternal life."

I love You, Lord Jesus, my Rock, my Strength!

I would never have given my life for the Lord, but Lord Jesus went out of His Way to die for a sinner like me, for someone who would not do the same for Him at the time!

Lord Jesus did all of the right things for someone like me who would have done the wrong things to Him.

Lord Jesus loved me, while I hated Him without reason. I was mad and upset at God, had my fist balled up, but He reached His hand down on me. I never had peace a day in my life until Lord Jesus came into my life and my heart. I just love Who He is! Bless you, Lord Jesus!

"Love one another as I have loved you," is what Lord Jesus commands us to do. Let us aim to please our Lord Jesus Christ. We can definitely do better; God knows we can.

Love one another!

Chapter 7
The Father, the Son, and the Holy Ghost

Bless You, Father God, Lord Jesus Christ His One and Only Son, and the Holy Spirit! All honor, glory, and praise go to You.

In 1 John 5:7 (KJV), brother John writes, "For there are Three that bear record in Heaven, the Father, the Word [Jesus Christ], and the Holy Ghost, and these Three are One."

In Deuteronomy 6:4, brother Moses said, "Hear, O Israel: The Lord our God, the Lord is One."

In 1 Corinthians 8:6, brother Paul writes, " ... yet for us there is but One God, the Father, from Whom all things came and for Whom we live; and there is but One Lord, Jesus Christ, through Whom all things came and through Whom we live."

All things came through God our Father and His Son Jesus Christ, and we live through God our Father and His Son Jesus Christ. How is all of this done? It is done by God's Spirit, The Holy Ghost, the Spirit of Truth.

In Zechariah 4:6, an angel told brother Zechariah, " ... This is the word of the Lord to Zerubbabel: 'Not by might nor by power, but by My Spirit,' says the Lord Almighty."

In John 6:63, Lord Jesus says to His disciples, "The Spirit gives life; the flesh counts for nothing. The Words I have spoken to you—they are full of the Spirit and life."

The Spirit gives Life. Jesus is the Way, the Truth, and the Life that the Spirit gives to whoever believes by faith in Jesus Christ, the Living Word of God, The Word of the Lord. Anytime God our Father has spoken to anyone in any way, it has always been through Jesus Christ—the Word—and Lord Jesus Christ operates through the Holy Spirit.

In John 6:44-45, Lord Jesus tells the Jews:

"No one can come to Me unless the Father who sent Me draws them, and I will raise them up at the last day. It is written in the Prophets: 'They will all be taught by God.' Everyone who has heard the Father and learned from Him comes to Me."

How is all of this done? It is done by the Holy Spirit, the Gift of God, the Living Waters, as brother John explains in John 7:37-39, when Jesus tells His disciples on the last day of the Festival of the Tabernacles:

> " ... 'Let anyone who is thirsty come to me and drink. Whoever believes in Me, as Scripture has said, rivers of living water will flow from within them.' By this He meant the Spirit, whom those who believed in Him were later to receive. Up to that time the Spirit had not been given, since Jesus had not yet been glorified."

In John 4:10, Jesus tells a Samaritan woman, "If you knew the Gift of God and Who it is that asks you for a drink, you would have asked Him and he would have given you Living Water."

But when the Samaritan woman asks Lord Jesus to give her the water, He tells her to call her husband despite the fact she never mentioned having a relationship with anyone. Now, she did not have a husband, and was, in fact, sleeping with a man who was not her husband, committing adultery, and the Lord Jesus knew it. Because of this, the woman recognizes Him as a prophet and speaks about the coming of the Messiah. At this point, Jesus tells her in John 4:26, "I, the one speaking to you—I am He."

In telling the Samaritan woman He is the Messiah, Lord Jesus is bringing her into the Light so she could receive the Living Water when It arrived at Pentecost. And because she told others in her town about Lord Jesus, they were curious. They wanted to see for themselves.

So, as brother John records in John 4:40-41, " ... when the Samaritans came to Him, they urged Him to stay with them, and He stayed two days. And because of His words many more became believers."

More sinners were being brought into the Light in preparation for the arrival of the Living Water.

Of course, the people at that time did not yet know anything about this Living Water, despite the fact It had always been present, from the Beginning, as we are told in Genesis 1:1-2: "In the beginning God created the heavens and the earth. Now the earth was formless and empty, darkness was over the surface of the deep, and the Spirit of God was hovering over the waters."

The Living Water, The Holy Ghost, The Holy Spirit, The Spirit of God has always been present from the Beginning of Creation.

Bless you, Father God, Lord Jesus Christ, and Holy Spirit!

We cannot come to Jesus Christ unless the Father, Who sent Jesus, sends the Holy Spirit to draw us to God and guide us to Jesus. The Holy Spirit has always been overseeing God's work. He is the Gift of God. He draws us to God our Father and guides us to Jesus Christ. It is the Holy Spirit Who leads us.

In Romans 8:14, brother Paul writes, "For those who are led by the Spirit of God are the Children of God."

In Exodus 13:21, brother Moses records the presence of the Spirit of God on their journey out of Egypt: "By day the Lord went ahead of them in a pillar of cloud to guide them on their way and by night in a pillar of fire to give them light, so that they could travel by day or night."

This pillar of cloud and pillar of fire were the Holy Spirit guiding them. The Holy Spirit is quite often represented by fire, both in the Old Testament and the New Testament:

Burning bush (Exodus 3:2)

Light and guidance (Exodus 13:21; Numbers 9:14-15, 17-23)

God's judgment (Numbers 11:1; 2 Kings 1:10, 12)

God's power (Judges 13:20; 1 Kings 18:38)

Cleansing sin (Psalms 66:10; Proverbs 17:3)

Tongues of fire (Acts 2:3-4)

Consuming fire (Hebrews 12:29)

In the form of fire, the Holy Spirit brings us God's presence, God's passion, and God's purity[9]. The Holy Spirit guides us to our Father God and to our Lord Jesus Christ.

In John 14:15-17, Lord Jesus says to His disciples on the evening of His betrayal:

> "If you love me, keep my commands. And I will ask the Father, and He will give you another Advocate to help you and be with you forever—the Spirit of Truth. The world cannot accept Him, because it neither sees Him nor knows Him. But you know Him, for He lives with you and will be in you."

That same evening, Lord Jesus reassures His disciples in John 16:13-14:

> "But when He, the Spirit of Truth, comes, He will guide you into all the truth. He will not speak on His own; He will speak only what He hears, and He will tell you what is yet to come. He will glorify Me because it is from Me that He will receive what He will make known to you."

You see, the Holy Spirit glorifies—and leads us to—Jesus and He tells us what is yet to come. The Holy Spirit teaches us, as we read in John 16:8-11 about the Advocate Jesus will send after His death:

> "When He comes, He will prove the world to be in the wrong about sin and righteousness and judgment: about sin, because people do not believe in Me [Jesus]; about righteousness, because I am going to the Father, where you can see Me no longer; and about

judgment, because the prince of this world [Satan] now stands condemned."

The Holy Spirit teaches us about sin, righteousness, and judgment through Jesus Christ, the Living Word of God. He teaches us daily as we put our hope, love, and faith in Jesus Christ, and seals us with a Mark, as Paul writes in Ephesians 1:11-14:

> "In Him [Jesus Christ] we were also chosen, having been predestined according to the plan of Him [God the Father] Who works out everything in conformity with the purpose of His will, in order that we, who were the first to put our hope in Christ, might be for the praise of His glory. And you also were included in Christ when you heard the message of truth, the gospel of your salvation. When you believed, you were marked in Him with a seal, the promised Holy Spirit, Who is a deposit guaranteeing our inheritance until the redemption of those who are God's possession—to the praise of His glory."

The moment we truly believe, we are marked with a Seal: the promised Holy Spirit!

The Holy Spirit draws us to God our Father and guides us to Jesus Christ; Jesus Christ fills us and baptizes us in the Holy Spirit with fire. Then the Holy Spirit lives with us—He lives *in* us!

All this is by God's grace that comes through Jesus Christ. In John 1:16-17, brother John said, "Out of His fullness we have received grace in place of grace already given. For the Law came through Moses; grace and truth came through Jesus Christ."

In Ephesians 2:8-9, Paul writes, "For it is by grace you have been saved, through faith—and this is not from yourselves, it is the gift of God—not by works, so that no one can boast."

Grace is a gift of God; grace is how we are saved—through faith, not from ourselves. It all comes from God our Father. No one can say, "I saved myself!"

It was the Holy Spirit Who had the grace to give that led me to the Word of God, and the Word of God led me to God our Father, who had the grace to send Jesus Christ to me!

Jesus Christ fills us with the Holy Spirit daily through the faith we have in Him as we continue to put our trust in Him. All this is wonderful! Without the Holy Spirit, I cannot even understand God my Father or Jesus Christ, His One and Only Son, my Lord and Savior. Without the Holy Spirit, nothing that comes from God our Father or the Lord Jesus Christ will ever make any sense to us, because everything God our Father and the Lord Jesus Christ say to do is only perceived—discerned—through the Holy Spirit.

In 1 Corinthians 2:14, brother Paul writes:

> "The person without the Spirit does not accept the things that come from the Spirit of God but considers them foolishness, and cannot understand them because they are discerned only through the Spirit."

We need the Holy Spirit to see the Lord Jesus, as the Bible says in Hebrews 12:14: " ... without holiness no one will see the Lord."

This holiness comes from our Lord Jesus Christ by putting our faith and trust in Him, by loving Him with all our heart, soul, and mind, and by being obedient to His Words, Commands, and Commandments with all our heart, soul, and mind. He does not ask us to be perfect—just to be obedient from our heart, and He will make us holy through our obedience to His Word.

In Leviticus 20:8, the Lord God said, "Keep My decrees and follow them. I am the Lord, Who makes you holy."

As Jesus tells His disciples in John 14:15, "If you love Me, keep My commands." The Lord Jesus gives us the Holy Spirit through our faith in God's Word, the Lord Jesus Christ, the Living Word of God. He always has and always will. Brother Caleb had the Holy Spirit in the Old Testament while he was out in the wilderness with Moses for over 40 years as the Lord said in Numbers 14:24:

> "But because My servant Caleb has a different Spirit [the Holy Spirit] and follows Me wholeheartedly, I will bring him into the land he went to, and his descendants will inherit it."

Caleb waited over 40 years to inherit this land. But Caleb held on to God's Word for all of those 40 years and God our Father blessed him for his obedience, even kept up his strength all those years. Caleb was 40 years old when God promised him the land, and he was 85 when he went in and took possession of it as God promised. If we keep God's Word, He will give us the Holy Spirit. If we repent at God's Word, He will pour out the Holy Spirit to us through Jesus Christ, Who Himself is the Living Word of God.

In Proverbs 1:23, the Lord said through brother Solomon:

> "Repent at My rebuke!

THE FATHER, THE SON, AND THE HOLY GHOST

Then I will pour out My thoughts to you,

I will make known to you My teachings."

The Lord our God gives the Holy Spirit to all who believe in God's Word, to whoever submits to God's Word, and to all to have regard for Him. He draws us through the Holy Spirit, and the Holy Spirit leads us and guides us to Jesus Christ. Jesus Christ Himself will one days return and lead us and guide us to God our Father Who dwells in an unapproachable Light.

AMEN!

THANK YOU, FATHER GOD FOR YOUR GRACE, YOUR MERCY,
AND YOUR LOVE;
THANK YOU, JESUS CHRIST, MY LORD AND SAVIOR, MY GOD AND FRIEND,
WHO SUFFERED, DIED, WAS BURIED, AND ROSE AGAIN
SO WE SINNERS WHO BELIEVE IN HIM SHALL HAVE ETERNAL LIFE;
THANK YOU, HOLY SPIRIT, MY TEACHER AND GUIDE, WHO BRINGS US
OUR FATHER GOD'S PRESENCE, PASSION, AND PURITY SO THAT WE MAY
UNDERSTAND!

Notes & References

[1]Cline, Austin. "Muslim View of the Ten Commandments." *www.LearnReligions.com*. Learn Religions, 27 Aug 2020. Web. 27 May 2023. https://www.learnreligions.com/muslim-view-of-the-ten-commandments-250914.

[2]Wikipedia contributors. "Arishdavargas." *Wikipedia, The Free Encyclopedia*. Wikipedia, The Free Encyclopedia, 16 Apr 2023. Web. 24 May 2023.

[3]Wikipedia contributors. "Moksha." *Wikipedia, The Free Encyclopedia.* Wikipedia, The Free Encyclopedia, 11 Jun 2023. Web. 20 Jun 2023.

[4]"What is the Egyptian Book of the Dead?" *www.GotQuestions.org*. Web. 25 May 2023. https://www.gotquestions.org/Egyptian-Book-of-the-Dead.html

[5]Mark, Joshua J. "The Negative Confession." *World History Encyclopedia*. World History Encyclopedia, 27 Apr 2017. Web. 23 May 2023.

[6]Mark, Joshua J. "The Egyptian Afterlife & The Feather of Truth." *World History Encyclopedia*. World History Encyclopedia, 30 Mar 2018. Web. 27 May 2023.

[7]GreekMythology.com Editors. "The Seven Deadly Sins." *GreekMythology.com.* GreekMythology.com, 02 Dec. 2022. Web. 21 Jun 2023.

[8]Wikipedia contributors. "Salvation." *Wikipedia, The Free Encyclopedia*. Wikipedia, The Free Encyclopedia, 26 May 2023. Web. 28 May 2023.

[9]"How is the Holy Spirit like a fire?" *www.GotQuestions.org*. Web. 14 Jun 2023. https://www.gotquestions.org/Holy-Spirit-fire.html

About the Author:
Davante Farmer

A resident of Lynchburg, Virginia, Davante Farmer's life has been a mixture of some good days, many bad days, and a good dose of hardship. But even when things seemed hopeless, the light of Jesus Christ shone through to his family with the help of his great-grandmother, whom he credits for teaching him what it means to honor God. With her love, encouragement, and inspiration, Davante earned his G.E.D., turned away from the evil that trapped him, and focused his mind, heart, and soul on the glorious grace of God. And while he is the first to admit he is an imperfect man and a sinner by nature, he is also blessed to be a vessel used by God to spread the Good News that is Jesus.

Connect with Davante:
Facebook: https://facebook.com/va.dontsleep.1
YouTube: https://www.youtube.com/@davantefarmer7854
Email: davantefarmer6@gmail.com

"Rebuilding with the Cornerstone"
Acts 4:10-12 (WEB)

" ... may it be known to you all, and to all the people of Israel, that in the name of Jesus Christ of Nazareth, whom you crucified, whom God raised from the dead, this man stands here before you whole in Him. He is 'the stone which was regarded as worthless by you, the builders, which has become the head of the corner.' There is salvation in no one else, for there is no other name under heaven that is given among men, by which we must be saved!"